MANCHESTER UNITED

Peter Leigh

Published in association with The Basic Skills Agency

Hodder Murray

A MEMBER OF THE HODDER HEADLINE GROUP

The Publishers would like to thank the following for permission to reproduce copyright material:

Photo credits
p.iv, 10, 20 © Coloursport; pp.4, 17 © PA Photos; p.23 © All Action; p.26 © Michael Steele/Getty Images; p.28 © Rex Features.

Orders: please contact Bookpoint Ltd, 130 Milton Park, Abingdon, Oxon OX14 4SB. Telephone (44) 01235 827720. Fax: (44) 01235 400454. Lines are open from 9.00–5.00, Monday to Saturday, with a 24-hour message answering service. You can also order through our website www.hoddereducation.co.uk

Cover photo: © John Peters/Manchester United via Getty Images
Typeset in 14pt Palatino by SX Composing DTP, Rayleigh, Essex.
Printed in Great Britain by CPI Bath.

A catalogue record for this title is available from the British Library

ISBN-10 0 340 90073 3
ISBN-13 978 0 340 90073 4

Contents

Matt Busby and the Busby Babes.
Manchester v Aston Villa. FA Cup Final, 1957.

1 The Busby Babes

The sky was grey.
Snow covered the airport.

On the runway the snow was starting to melt
and turn to slush,
but more snow was coming.

The captain looked through the windscreen,
and thought about taking off.

He had already tried twice.
Both times he had failed.

The big plane was full.
On board were sports writers, photographers
and football fans.
And there was also
the most famous football team in the world.

Manchester United!

Everybody was talking about them.
They were so young and fresh and exciting.
They had already won the League twice.
Many of them were teenagers,
and the captain was only 28.

That's why they were called the Busby Babes,
after their manager Matt Busby.
They were all star players –
Tommy Taylor, Duncan Edwards
and, especially, the new star Bobby Charlton.

He had scored two goals in the match that day.
They had beaten Red Star Belgrade,
and were now in the semi-final
of the European Cup.
That was Matt Busby's dream –
to win the European Cup.
If they did,
they would be the first British club
ever to win it.

Everybody was sure they could.
The Busby Babes!
They were brilliant.

The captain looked at the runway again.
Perhaps he shouldn't try again.
But he had only stopped for more fuel.
The team was tired
and keen to get home.
They had another important match on Saturday.

The sports writers were keen to get home too.
They had to write their stories for the papers.

And the fans too –
they were keen to get home,
so they could tell everybody about the game.

The captain eased the plane on to the runway.
He would try once more.

The plane roared along the runway.
The tail-lights disappeared
into the snow and darkness.

But the plane never took off.

The Munich air crash, 6 February 1958.

The snow and slush slowed the plane down
so it couldn't take off.
It skidded off the runway,
and smashed through a fence.
It crashed into a house,
and burst into flames.

Twenty-three people died,
including eight Manchester United players.

The Busby Babes were no more.
But the legend of Manchester United was born.

2 The New Babes

The Munich air crash was on
6 February 1958,
the blackest day in the history of
Manchester United.

When the news reached England,
people cried in the streets.
They gathered round the radio or television
listening to the list of dead and injured.
Everyone loved the Busby Babes.

Matt Busby was the worst injured.
For months he couldn't move.
When he finally went back to Manchester,
thousands of people cheered him in the streets.

They felt sorry for him.
They thought he was brave,
but they thought he was finished.

They were wrong!

While he was in hospital for all that time
Matt Busby had decided to start again.
He would build another Manchester United,
a second Busby Babes.
And they would be even better than the first.
And this time they would win
the European championship!

He began to build his new team
around the players who had survived Munich,
especially Bobby Charlton.

Bobby Charlton was a wonderful player.
He had a swerve that could fool a whole team,
and a left-foot shot that could score goals
from 40 metres.
His brother Jack was also a footballer.

Soon Manchester United began to win again.
They were even in the Cup Final
the same year as Munich!

In 1962, Matt Busby brought Denis Law
to Old Trafford.
He was a Scot,
but had been playing in Italy.
He had a shock of blond hair
and was razor-sharp near the goal.

Denis Law started to score
and in 1963 they won the FA Cup.
Everyone was talking about
Bobby Charlton and Denis Law.

But then in 1963,
a slim, black-haired, young Irishman
played his first game for Manchester United.
Soon he would be more famous
than even Bobby Charlton and Denis Law.
Soon he would be the greatest player
in English football and,
some say, in the world.
His name was George Best.

3 George Best

There was a magic about George Best.
Millions of people watched Manchester United
just to see him.
And they still remember the games he played in
and the things he did.

The things he did seemed impossible.
You couldn't believe what you were seeing.

He would twist and turn,
left and right,
backwards and forwards.
The ball seemed stuck to his feet.
He would go around defenders,
between defenders,
and through defenders.

The magic of George Best.
Manchester United v Crystal Palace, 1971.

He would be in the corner of the field,
with three defenders around him.
Suddenly he would be past them,
with his shirt outside his shorts,
and the ball still at his feet.
The defenders were left standing there,
looking at each other,
feeling silly.

How did he do that?
Nobody could do that.
But George Best could!

Or he would play the ball
off the legs of the defenders.
You thought it was just luck,
until he did it again . . .
and again!

Then he would shoot from a crazy position,
and the ball would swerve into the net.

It was impossible.
Nobody could score like that.
But George Best did!

The crowds would watch
with their mouths open.
They could not believe
what they had just seen.
And then the roars and shouts and claps
would roll around the ground.
George Best had done it again.

What made him so good?

He was small.
He looked thin and weak.
But he wasn't.
He was wiry
and much stronger than he looked.

He was nimble and very quick
and always kept his eyes on the ball,
just in front of his toes.
He never even seemed to look up.

But perhaps you can't explain it.
Perhaps it was just genius!

He wasn't just a football star.
He was more like a pop star,
or a film star.
He drove fast cars,
had famous girlfriends,
and threw all-night parties at expensive clubs.
His picture was always in the papers,
or in the magazines,
or on the television.
Girls screamed when he ran on to the pitch.
They mobbed his car,
and camped outside his house.

He was the first football superstar!

4 Europe

Manchester United was again
the best team in England.
They won the Cup once
and the League twice.
And then in 1968
they got to the final of the European Cup.

It was just ten years after Munich –
ten years after the death of the Busby Babes.

Everyone knew
what this match meant for Matt Busby.

Bobby Charlton said afterwards,
'It was our duty.
It had become a family thing.'
He had been at Munich too.

The final was at Wembley.
It was against Benfica.
It was a tight, hard game.
United were leading 1–0 for most of the game.
Then Benfica equalised in the last few minutes.
This would mean extra time.

The United players sat down
in the centre of the pitch.
They looked tired out.
Matt Busby moved quietly among them,
talking to each one,
trying to inspire them,
to urge them on.

5 Sir Matt Busby

It was a cold, grey day in Manchester.
The shops had closed early.
The traffic had stopped.
The streets were full, but quiet.
The people were standing in silence
as a funeral passed slowly through them –
the funeral of Sir Matt Busby.

All the old players were there,
including George Best and Bobby Charlton
(now Sir Bobby Charlton).
But standing with them were new players,
like Ryan Giggs and Eric Cantona,
and a new manager – Alex Ferguson.

6 Alex Ferguson

Under Alex Ferguson, Manchester United
has won the Premiership seven times.
The team has won the FA Cup four times.
And it has won the League Cup,
the European Cup,
the European Cup Winners' Cup,
and the European Super Cup.
No other team has a record like it.

Why is Manchester United so good?
Some say it's the fans.
Some say it's the money,
because Manchester United is very rich.
But if you ask the players,
they say simply that it's the manager.

Alex Ferguson holding the Carling Premiership trophy in 1996.

Like many great managers,
Alex Ferguson is a Scot.
And like them, he learned his football
in a tough school.

Winning is all-important –
there are no prizes for losers.
He gives 100 per cent to the club,
and expects no less from the players.
There are no excuses.
And if Alex thinks a player
is not trying his hardest,
or is past his best,
then he is out,
no matter how famous he is.

But Alex is well-liked by the players
and by the staff.
He is kind and helpful,
and knows every one of them.
It is only those
who are not doing their best
who see the hard side of Alex Ferguson.

He has developed the youth sides
and the training at Manchester United.
Both Ryan Giggs and Paul Scholes
started there as boys –
they have never played for another club.
But Alex has also brought in foreign players,
sometimes the best in the world.

The first was Eric Cantona.
He was a great player,
but could be moody and difficult.
In 1994, he was sent off for a foul.
As he was going, a man in the crowd
shouted something at him.
Eric went mad.
He ran and kicked at the man.
Then he was hurried off the field.

Millions saw it on television.
There were arguments about it
for days afterwards.
The papers went on and on about it.
The television showed it time and time again.
There were even arguments
in Parliament about it!

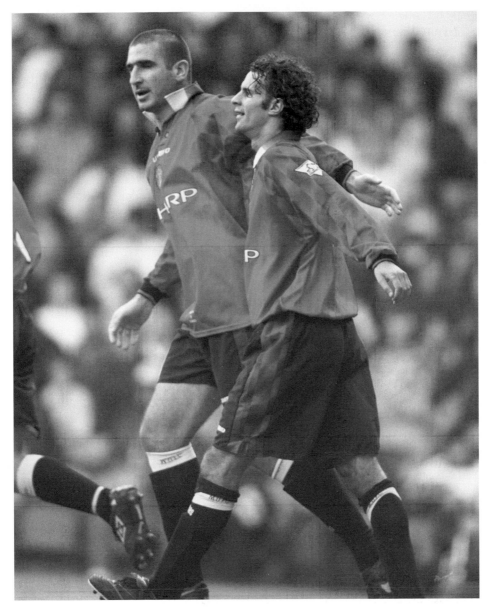

Two of the most famous players of 1996: Eric Cantona (left) and Ryan Giggs (right).

Should Eric be charged?
Should he be fined,
or imprisoned?
Should he be sent back to France?

In the end,
he was given Community Service,
and suspended from football.

It was a hard blow
for someone as proud as Eric.
But when he returned
he seemed better.
He was calmer,
and more in control of himself.

You could see this
in the FA Cup Final in 1996.
With nearly the last kick of the game,
Eric calmly scored the goal
that won the cup for Manchester.

7 The Team Today

When Alex started at Manchester United
he built a team around the captain,
Bryan Robson.
Bryan was a great player.
He was also captain of England,
but he had a terrible injury to his shoulder,
which stopped him playing his best.

The captain now is Roy Keane.
He's exactly the same as Alex.
He's strong and hard.
He never stops trying,
and only winning is good enough for him.

There are other stars around him –
Paul Scholes and Ryan Giggs,
and the wonder-boy of football – Wayne Rooney.

Wayne Rooney at Old Trafford, 2004.

Manchester United had a special year in 1999.
They had won the FA Cup and the Premiership.
They were in the final of the European Cup.
Could they win the treble?

The score was 1–0 against them
all the way through the match.
There were 90 seconds left.
Then suddenly Manchester United scored twice.
They had won!
It was incredible.
No other English team had won as much.
This new Manchester United
had won even more than the old one.

There could only be one reward.
Alex Ferguson, like Matt Busby before him,
became Sir Alex Ferguson.
By 2004, he had been in charge
of Manchester United for 18 years.
He is the longest serving manager in the world,
and for fans, the best.

What does the future hold for Manchester United?